Singing Forever in My Memories

Singing Forever in My Memories

Collected Poems and Vignettes

by

Michael J. Walsh

 **mosaic**PRESS

Library and Archives Canada Cataloguing in Publication

Title: Singing forever in my memories : collected poems and vignettes / by Michael J. Walsh.

Names: Walsh, Michael J., 1943- author.

Identifiers: Canadiana (print) 20230511783 |
             Canadiana (ebook) 20230511791 |

ISBN 9781771617369 (softcover) | ISBN 9781771617376 (PDF) |
ISBN 9781771617383 (EPUB) | ISBN 9781771617390 (Kindle)

Classification: LCC PS8645.A475 A6 2023 | DDC C811/.6—dc23

Published by Mosaic Press, Oakville, Ontario, Canada, 2023.

MOSAIC PRESS, Publishers
www.Mosaic-Press.com
Copyright © Michael Walsh, 2023

Printed and bound in Canada.

MOSAIC PRESS
1252 Speers Road, Units 1 & 2, Oakville, Ontario, L6L 5N9
(905) 825-2130 • info@mosaic-press.com • www.mosaic-press.com

Table of Contents

VIGNETTES
Reading Pictures and Seeing Words

Dedication

Now it is time for me to thank ALL those who welcomed me back into their lives, a solitary outsider, carrying only a bag of harmonic verses. I was told that I had not changed a bit after over fifty years away from home. A polite lie to say the least. But now it is time for me to share those memories filled with rhythmic stories of a still forever, wandering minstrel. Thank you.

An Introduction to the possible future of creative artist

Language is the most powerful influence on an individual's development because most of the other influences work through language. The character of a people is also determined as much by the character of its language as by its climate, its resources and its technologies. (MJW)

"The spoken & written forms of all languages differ markedly. Speech is loose, spontaneous and vanishes instantly. Made to last, writing is inherently more formal because it limits both the sound and meaning in order to communicate clearly. It cannot reproduce the almost infinite variety of live speech, for even using our new technologies experimentally, is really only the search for a new way to convey its meaning." (MJW)

"Artistic experience is creative insanity or controlled insanity. Perhaps some would say that Art is 'Needing the dough; for others it is 'Kneading the Dough to survive for another day. (MW) Albert Einstein said: "I believe in Imagination... it is more important than knowledge. " I suppose that artists need to consider how this quote affects their own creativity. (MJW)

"The proper function of a college is the imaginative acquisition of knowledge... Imagination is a contagious disease. It cannot be measured by the yard, or weighed by the pound and then delivered to the students by members of the Faculty. It can only be communicated by them, whose members themselves wear their learning with Imagination." (from Alfred North Whitehead in **The Aims of Education, 1929**) Does this opinion make educational sense for you in today's Arts & Media programs. Some have argued that learning the most recent software is the most important feature of your need to know in the future. Agree or disagree. (MW)

"..for us creativity should become the last magic in our materialist world and the modern artist is in his own way a magic hunter whose depth of feeling makes him lose all self-consciousness when he can identify with what he creates. These thoughts became part of George Woodcock's (RIP) approach to the development of Literature in Canada over the past 50 years. He also said that the artist/writer should not only represent but also identify with his subject. Do you agree with his opinion & how do you approach your own creativity? (MJW)

'*I want to oppose the idea that the school has to teach directly that special knowledge and those accomplishments which one has to use later directly in life. The school used to always have as its aim that the young person leave it as a harmonious personality, not as a specialist. This in my opinion is true in a certain sense even for technical schools, whose students will devote themselves to a quiet profession. The development of general ability for independent thinking and judgement should always be placed foremost, not the acquisition of special knowledge. If a person masters the fundamentals of his subject and has learned to think independently, he will surely find his way and besides will be better able to adapt himself to progressive changes than the person whose training principally consists in the acquiring of detailed knowledge. (Albert Einstein, **On Education**, 1936)* In my opinion Einstein's comments merit further attention. The debate at all levels in our market driven economy has convinced many that the Arts & Humanities courses and programs are a waste of time and frivolous, window dressing. However, I have noticed that the major new AI corporations have found that to stay profitable lay offs are affecting large numbers of Tech wizards, who don't know what to do when a saturated market of younger wizards appears at half the salary working the electronic highway.

I seem to remember seeing in a Business text book that words like: *Wage/Price, Profit/Loss; Supply/Demand* have not changed that much in Today's Global Economy, when governments are carrying huge debt loads to provide the basics to their unemployed masses, who are presented with the daily stories of Recession and Depression. Then the next generation of under-employed

Tech wizards are encouraged to go back to school to find a new beginning at rebuilding an ignored, crumbling infrastructure. (MJW)

Passion, for the artist suggests intensity, emotion, eloquence, desire, excitement and temperament. It is an active ingredient which captivates and captures the artist's attention and enables him to become an active participant in the exploration of the creative act.. It is exploratory, sensual, emotive, and imaginary with the hidden urge that drives him to FEEL OUT an artistic expression with urgency, love and care. It is the active ingredient in his make- up which enables him to devote his time and energy to the creative project. It is also the stumbling block to any creativity when the urgency to create loses its lustre and the energy dissipates. For an artist this is expressed through his own uncertainty concerning his own creations or through the public's rejection of his art. It is always the artist's challenge to decide whether the battle is worth the effort." (MJW)

Now you can seek an answer from your own life & experience. Do you care or are you too busy to take the time? Perhaps the poet, Tennyson told us what to do in a line from his poem Ulysses: To strive, to seek, to find, and not to yield. *"The existence of words or symbols for absent things enables human beings into situations which do not actually exist. This gift is the imagination, and it is simple and strong, for it is no more than the human ability to make images in the mind and use them to construct imaginary situations. We do a great harm to children in their education when we accustom them to separate reason from imagination, simply for the convenience of the school timetable. For imagination is not confined to wild bursts of fantasy. Imagination is the manipulation inside the mind of absent things, by using their place-images or words or symbols... it is always an experimental process. (Jacob Bronowski,* **The Visionary Eye***, 1978)*

"There are universal shapes to which everybody is subconsciously conditioned and to which they can respond if their conscious control does not shut them off.

(Henry Moore, Sculpture: **Form & Shape**)

FINALLY

Do you remember going to the beach as a child & searching for pebbles, bones, shells, rocks, seaweed? I do, and according to Moore the observation of Nature is part of an artist's life (just add yourself to the list too) because it enlarges his form-knowledge, keeps him fresh and from working only by formula and feeds inspiration." Do you enjoy some peaceful time taking a walk in a local park, smelling the flowers, watching a squirrel scurry or some birds chirping. Nature at work and you are part of Nature. Take care of it and yourself. (MJW)

Mike Walsh, June 2023,
Oakville, Ontario

Poems

Galactic Dreams

I am the fetal fusion,
I am the electric glow.
I am the consummate beginning
Of my parents' devouring embrace.
I am their bodies
Entwined,
Combined
Refined.

Now I am ME
Savouring and seeking
The flavours and perfumes
Of my IM
Mortality.
Forever meandering along
The crowded streets
And journeys in my life.

Still I muse
Within my declining frame
That I will soar on thunderbird's wings
Beyond Vincent's "Starry Night"
And
Glide to galaxies
That Orbit and Collide
With fission and fusion
"Ad infinitum"
Before landing at last
In that peaceful place
Called home.

Life's journey is a river

I am a gentle river,
I am still, I am calm,
I trickle and I shine,
I sparkle and I smile.
I feed the floral fields,
I bless the golden harvests.

I am the music in the stream.
I am its echo
Sending everlasting harmonies
To the windswept breezes
That caress the scented pines
Along the endless shore.

I am the turbines of change,
I am the grist of grain,
I fill the fishermen's nets
I mingle 'midst the rocks
That nestle in the soft, wet sand.

I follow the wind that blows,
I am the air that flows
Through flapping, canvas sheets.
I am the current set adrift
Ambling across the land,
Furrowing in the crevices,
Cascading over cliffs.

I am the river of chances,
I am the river of changes.
I am the endless mover
The never-ending provocateur.

I am the journey begun
With the paddles lapping,

The sails clapping,
The engines chugging,

I am angry, I am thunder.
I am lightning,
I tumble and I fall,
Gnashing and gashing
Against the tranquil shore.
I am out of control
I am rushing, I am crushing,
Roaring at my world.

But then
I am alone.
I am the river of truth
I am the virtuous gift
I am blessed with hope
I am filled with life.
I am love, I am happiness
I have no regrets.
I am massive, I am small
I am a drip, I am a drizzle
I am the thunder, I am the storm
Berating the friendly shore.

I am the waves and their return
I am one with the sandy dunes
I have reached my goal,
I love my soul.

I believe...
I am honest, I am true
I live in silence
To find peaceful repose
I am faithful to a dream
I cling to hope.

I am charity, I want to share
I give what I can take,

I take what I can give
I want to live.
I am the river of virtue,
I am the river of change

I am its flow,
I am its current
Meandering at will
But always constant
Even when I am alone.

I am the universal friend
Living with the ebb and flow.
Wishing to wash away the pain
That lingers still in a deserted
brain.

I am the Oasis,
I am the life Refreshing your thirsty soul,
For I am your journey
To a distant shore
Where you are not alone

Sketches at Hermans Island

Shadows and shingles
whining in brine, while willows wilt
and whither beneath whistling winds
whooshing roars on rocky shores
Spraying and flaying,
Gulls wings swinging in draft
And drift on dune
Sand shore amidst
Weedy sea crusted crabs
Clamming ready for
Steam chowder pots
While bobbing nets call
Cod and flounder
To come a grounder
Milking their way into
Onion and potato broth

A trail of rushes hewn down in toil
Brittle soil leading to windy sails
With mast high wires rattling
tales in the face of a gale,
capping the anchor in froth and chop

Evening Tide
Still lament of schooner
Resting in murky harbour
Womb whence splashing
Gulls disturb the
Croaking dusk of cricket
Thrushes calling songs
Bringing home to
Nest the rumbling boats
Pushing aside the
The wavy glass of

Still salt water
On low tide slime and sandy
Shell driftwood.

Flickering beacons lighting
Hay dry green and
Red roof bam while
Inky blue with gathering hue
Comes to rest along
The harbour shore.

Soft magic trees melting
Into sleep washed with
Breezy skies that tickle
My dreams and leave me
Tingly warm before
Resting outside my window
In silent stillness
'Til the break of dawn.

The Summer Races

Hazy heat of summer
Air pushing jib sails
Across a sparkling inlet
So fair with
Slashed vermilion, white
Fluttering, strung to a
Rudder where a dashing
Yellow, green opposes it
In the bay.

Dancing, prancing ballet
Boats chasing
Butterflies and bees
Across the meadows
Where darting swallows
Wing in purple swoop
A round the broken ricks
And weather beaten barns

Lyiing in disarray
With mangled pots
And hoes and rusty rakes
Leaning in cobweb dust and
Stony dampness on the floor,
Heirlooms, hung from nails
Along the walls by
Pioneers' hands long since gone.

Then emerging to savour the
Sungolden grass,
With the boats chasing phantoms
Across the rippling, rainbow bay
Content to stay and race
Until the end of day.

Morning Fog
Wet, misty, foggy morning dew
Shakes through my bones now
Squishing the spongy, popping
Seaweed shore where
Remnants rest in clusters
On the sand.
There some
Glassy gems once
Vessels for ale and gin
Or ginger beer
And there some
Porcelain pieces of
Pink and blue
Now teacups for the
Salt watery sea

Past a rust masted hull
Leaning in a senile
Sleep on the high dry bank
And onto wharf where
Whooping boys just offshore
Sail in line between

Anchored masts of Schooner,
Shark and Cod Bank fleets
Afloat in foggy sleep.

Then to sit and grin
In friendly accord
with a gentle man
with time to leave
his work alone
and talk.

The Ovens National Park

Rough resounding roars
Ring over rocky shores
Calling the visitor to explore
The cavernous oven lairs
Where shingle dragons
Spew their salty spray
Over clinging weeds
And sinewy veins
While Neptune's trumpets blare
And echo in the chamber
With Cerberus barking like thunder
At the door
Tempting young Argonauts to come
Closer to his gnaw.

Overhead a swooping gull
Glides through windy drafts
Alone and free.

The cliffs like biscuit ginger
Drip with time,
While far at sea
A fog horn wails a
Cool and lingering note
to summer crews
That yearn for home.

Lunenburg, Nova Scotia

A horn screaming from afar
Sounds the noonday break
With sturdy painted timbers
Soaring skyward from fog laced streets
While touring gnomes roam
In search of soup and souvenirs.

Lunenburg, Nova Scotia
Where amiable, street corner people
Amble and josh in
Lingering groups outside
Drugstore, Post Office
and Foodliner store
puffing pipes filled with
tales and memories
of yesteryear
when Schooners jammed
the waterside street
just down the way

Now a floating museum
decked in tourist fashion
welcoming the holiday army
to snap 3x5 memories
for the folks back home.

Up above the solid timbers
Stand alone and true
As Lunenburg greets
The sun again at noon
And amiable pipes linger still
Outside drugstore, Post Office
And Foodliner store
With tales and memories
Of yesteryear
When Schooners jammed
The waterside street
Just down the way.

Maritime Madness

Crazy weather!
What shall I wear?
I turn my head for a raincoat
And find
You told the sun
To pour out
From where, I'll never know, .
Why won't you share?
Up and down,
Down and up
I prance and skip.
Give me fog glasses
In case it shines.
I'll even wear rubber boots
To pick strawberries by.
Crazy, windy, shifty
Weather clown!
Throwing water buckets
Filled with air
To test and tease
My imaginings.
What's next?
Does it snow in July
Or are those really reindeer
Pulling a lobster pot
Across the sandy sea
In July that
I think, I see?

More Maritime Madness

Snaking down the road
Past Riverport's friendly steeple
Past bam and fisherman's shack,
Bobbing, blue dory,
Solitary, cow cudding
And seashore cemetery
At last I meet a sign:
NEXT LEFT

GLADEES CANTEEN
3M.

Thank God, says I
As a wagon from BC
Coughs up some dust
Going down the road
The other way.
I hurtle on by
Intent, at least, to have
My blanket on the beach
By three.
Then I arrive and see
A foggy canteen,
A pounding sea,
Some whistling sand
And me.

Be damned, says I
And hurtle on out
To catch BC.

Blue Rocks
Imagine,
I saw you on a postcard
And didn't believe
But sure enough
You're there
Shack by shack,
Trap upon trap,
Green and red,
Yellow and gold
With slate blue rocks
Sliced like bread,
Corrugated chairs for
Mighty gulls who
Dine on crabs and clams,
Sea urchins and peanut butter jam.

Safe haven for the fishing fleet
Standing the tides of time,
You unfold your arms
To huddled buffs with
Paints and brushes
Eagerly watering in
The salty lines of a
White framed church
With a four-square steeple
And a red chimney
Running up one side.

But for me you are much more
Than a coloured photo
Found in a tourist's travel brochure.

Music

Bagpipes wailing,
Blow notes across oceans of dreams
Alive in the eternal silence
Of far away memories.
Feeling the salt spray of centuries
Whispering through my hair
In rivulets of palm tree sway
On a warm azure, lemon-melon day
Releasing me from icy days of
Brittle fragility
Beside pounding Cambrian shores
Where trappers once slaved
To bring furs to lingering ladies
Bathed in glass houses,
While footmen waited.

Spring fling

Fiddleheads, flounders
Lobsters, grounders
Fishing spring
Buds on branches
Mudglue floods
Spring way
Song of the jay
Sappy ooze
That hummingbirds woo
Mothers suckled
Bee
Honey suckle
Rose round window
Wind with vine
And ivy
Sky, pie, lie
Sun skinned sublime
Orange and lime

Flashing flesh
Silk on silt
Salt savouring
Warm residue

Earth bursting spring
Bubbling breakfast ring
Sizzle and sing
Picture pitcher of
Buttermilk pouring
Cool and souring On
calico table Cloth
curtains Rippling
against Windows
wide Open fields
With children playing at

Pole dance way
And swaying away
Stroking sun fun
On a verdant carpet run
'Midst lily, tulip, crocus petals
Metal
Breezes shining on
Swinging swallows Winging
In turns upturned
Above the dove
In prayers of praise
For **love**

Memories

When I'm laid to rest
Beside brittle leaves
Covering the rainbow trail
Of windswept days

Let the crackling logs of home
Reveal me
Running through asphalt forests
Swinging my bat
And cracking the days away
In innocent abandon.

Before going to sleep
With chocolate tin soldiers
And ice cream trucks
Riding over billiard table
Fields and rubber chestnut
Trees with fruit
Bouncing along
My golden days.

Oh! To savour the salt spray
Of centuries roaring in
Choral confusion
Across the shingles
On the strand that's
Teased by time

Fragment

Blue ooze from
Reckless, restless
Thorny orange spikes
With straw birds cavorting
On turquoise carpet fens

Rhapsody in Blue

Blow your dreams slowly across my wrinkled brow on wet afternoons and helping me to recall my memories:

of prancing horses that pulled wagons filled with rags and old iron;

of milk horses that clopped along rattling pavements carrying white honey that flowed through my veins;

of coal faced Clydesdales pulling grimy bags that fed my warmth on cold winter's days;

of the curious cat that slivered along, spying the dog that stood beyond the lamp post which glistened silver by day and shone by night with a greenish yellow glow of security;

of the night when the stars burst forth and challenged the bats to retire behind the skeletal, bomb tom belfry of yesterday's peace.

and given a chance to travel on a magic carpet, I rose from my bed to discover the man beyond the moon, who ruled over all like the ding donging God that I met every Sunday;

a midnight man who rolled over the skies and carried me to new galaxies of peace and contentment.

Then the new day began with prancing horses and rattling milk bottles;

the music of bicycle bells ridden by my friends as they peddled their way to the red, brick house we called our school;

again the cats were sleeping contentedly on the sills of our sun smiling houses, buzzed by the bugs and butterflies;

And Mr.Rogers clomping out for his constitutional at the local pub to be refreshed by his daily pint.

Mulligan and Desmond Swing

Let me sing and fling out rainbows
As I jive and sway
Along the orange highway
Of stardust sparkles and
Catch a dashing bluebird flashing
In a ricket thicket hedge
Of candy floss petals

Blow me a note, a cool note
Show me jumping to your
Jazz ma' tazz
Razzle my ocean of turquoise glitter
And pounding bursts of shingle sunshine
Like nets of lace dripping
On my bronzed tranquility.

Or on the road again
To bouncy midway rides
That joyfully scream and shout
Above the roar of baseball scores
And games of chance
Where pink bunny rabbits
Wink back at me
With their winning scores.

Nocturnes

Soft as chenille fleece
Your haunting notes
Measuring my glide
Across an ocean
Of rhythmic chimes
Recalling nights
I have loved and lingered
Through
Consuming anew my soft
Awakenings
And
Calling the gentle breezes
To brush my desires
And
Live in harmony.

Drifting flowers arouse the urge
To snow with down on my brow
Comforting the lines of my concern
Over yesterday's dreams-
Visions of chance encounters
With mystics musing beside
The rivers and lotus pools
With garden birds singing
From silhouette branches
Smudged by a distant sun
Roaring at my tranquility,
But
Warning of storms to come
When I sang with
Harmony and joy

Bouncing raindrops dance off
Rocky walls and
Sing on roofs of

Amber and gold
Pitter pattering
On my window sill
Where elves dance
In my dreams
And dare the goblins to
Conclude a duet
Before giving peace
To my resolve.

Fragile tears slide slowly over
Your marble cheeks
Whispering gently to your lips
A rhapsody of
Idyllic passion that
Remains impressed for eternity

From neck to shoulder
And down
Salty pearls
caress your breasts
and
liquefy your thighs
before
Falling in a sparkling pool
at your feet
Like conclusions that smile
with time.

Sleep, oh sleep!
Go gently into that sweet night
That I may hug the hours
Of peace and dreams
That punctuate my journeys
Through corridors and laneways
Of chimneys and trees.
Then tempted to act
Upon a whim
I might stop to consider

My conclusions
Before old age fades
and
Leaves me only
Romantic illusions of yesterday

Heloise and Abelard

Oh!
Sweet Bride of Christ
Celibate solitude rests softly
On my soul
Like a weaver's thread
Waiting to be spun
For Him and Him alone
In celebration of tomorrow's morn
Yet now!
Like an arthritic pain
Viewed through a frame
Of splintered glass
I mourn upon a mattress
Of broken dreams
For you,
My Sweet Heloise.

Rebirth

Blood flow glowing
Mud glue slowing
Sinking in ooze.
Wispy winds
Rushing round robin
Red soil whence
Water washing away
Brittle brass leaves
Now new buds
Bursting to savour
Saviour celebrated eggs
Rolling down bell
Chiming hills singing
Praises for glow worms
Shining beneath
Windy trumpet skies.

The 1812 Overture

Turmoil and struggle crash like cymbals
On my migraine brain
Creating snakes and scorpions
That snarl and sting at
The breasts of nursing mothers.

Now change and pillage
Jangle through
Town and village
Slashing the chords of church bells
With the bloody music of their guns.
Futile protests fall before
Their savage swords
Lying now in crimson disarray
Upon the frozen ground.

Writing to the Music of the 1812 Overture on March 15, 1978

First draft: Hand written
Turmoil and struggle crash like cymbals on my migraine brain issuing forth snakes and scorpions that snarl and sting the peaceful bosoms of mothers who nurse their gentle innocents. Change and pillage jangle through village and town raping the sway of church bells and replacing them with the music of bloody cannons pulling apart the flesh of My Flesh. Futile protests fall before the savage sword and lie in bloody disarray on the frozen ground.

Turmoil and struggle
Crash like cymbals
On my migraine brain
Creating snakes and scorpions
That snarl and sting at
The breasts of nursing mothers.

Now change and pillage
Jangle through

Town and village
Slashing the chords of church bells
With the bloody music of their guns,
While futile protests fall before
The savage sword
And lie in crimson array
Upon the frozen ground.

NOTE: I have used this music frequently over the years to create a rhythmic language we call Poetry. If my imagination had gone in a different direction, it could have become Prose, Drama, Film or a combination of styles.

Could the word **Chords** become **Cords** in your opinion? I wonder.

Then I was just a Dreamer

For buried within
The silence of those cloistered bells
Where memories lingered still
Tranquil harmonies resonated.
Along the empty corridors
I abandoned years ago,
Echoing the hopes and dreams
I believed, I would receive

Now I hear a new raucous chorus
Arousing those hopes and dreams
I believe, I must retrieve
Before I land at last
In that peaceful place
Called home

FLUX

I am a flume of flaming liquid fire
Fuming after fame before
Igniting another frenzied time
Of endless struggle
Filling the troubling trivialities
Of my turmoil and trials
Hiding those tragic truths
That remain forever.
Inside my head,
The endless passionate pleas
With frozen brutality always
Raging and Raving
With Fear and Loathing before
Reframing my never-ending dreams.

Flying

Oh!
Sharp pains
Like rifles rattling
Rained down with
April flames on winter days
Then cowbells rang
And kites sailed
Over rushing
Plains
m
w
i
n
d
i
n
g
w
a
v
e
s

The Age of Iron

Lady, lady lingering still
In steely silence
Forlorn and icy cold
Wrapped in a shroud that
Buries your past
And
Stifles your heart.

Now new lights and signals
Announce the whistle blows
Of iron maidens arriving on time
 For those
Lovers who keep a schedule
Of arrivals and departure
In icy silence
while the Pale Rider
devours your passion
From a brief encounter
On a one way ticket to
Nowhere.

Nostalgia

Let me share
The fond memories of yesteryear
When we laughed and played
Our love games
To the music of marching bands
And
Cheering crowds
While
Waiting eagerly for
The night rites to begin
With Mancini and Miller
By moonlight.

The Sentinel

The sentinel crow caws nightly
From its perch on a telegraph pole,
Solitary in its silhouette blackness
Surrounded by a crimson sunset sky.
It calls with squawking energy
For its army to fly
In a cacophonous symphony
Over our suburban sprawl,
Where industry, neon
And our manicured lawns
Seek some rest
Before awakening to
Another congested dawn.

Illusion

To catch a sparkle on
Your lips is like a fresh
Illusion reflected in a
Summer haze on a
Polluted highway
That's strewn with
Metallic roses.

Glistening chariots sweep you into
My deserted arms and
Laughing jackal's music screams
Endlessly back to the
Beseeched pronouncements of my
Love.
Clearly the sparkle is tarnished
And sour breath percolates
The brew laden lines along
My caffeinated brow.

Now fresh lips caress
Your active insanity
And pour away the hours
That remind you of yesterday's
Routine kiss
Of dutiful bliss.

Interlude

Your solemnity calms my insanity
On hostile afternoons that
Pound and prod me.
Once more the leaves of summer whisper
Before
A stainless steel sky penetrates
My mind with icicles of gloom.
Once more the rainbow flutter
Of a butterfly passes my eyes
Suggesting a meadow dance
Under breezy summer skies
With lovers consuming the petals
And perfumes of innocence
But
Now the sky is sharp and metal hue
And like a bird that flings its wings
I am soaring with the falcon
Through drafts of autumn
Above a crisp and frigid
Land that ignores my ride.
Then
Rushing and bursting past
The rumbling, fumbling clouds
I light upon a kiss
To calm my soul
Before my wings are tempted
To close and tumble
And fall

Charlie: The Crazy Crusader

You were
The knight of darkness
Who pedaled
His gaunt frame
Down drizzling streets
At midnight.
A blue eyed chevalier
Who brandished
The air
With a bicycle pump
And gestured insanely
About England, Germany
and
The madness of war.
They took you away as
The patron of windmills
Who was martyred
For peace.
Ignored
But NOT
Forgotten.

Lawrence of Arabia

Woven in contradiction
A bastard of Irish lineage
Who drew strength and pain
From the sands of a far off land
An Oxonian dwarf
Who savoured the whip of a boy
More than the praises of
Ministers, princes and kings.
A joyless, reckless introvert
Who sought solace
In silent flagellation
While lighting the Imperial flame of
England's shame.
A pocket book hero
Who hid behind
A mask of self deception
A conceited, arrogant perfectionist
Who with condescending grace
Consumed the dowagers' strawberries
And tea in Bloomsbury gardens
Before disappearing with hirsute haste
To a masochist's thrashing.
An anonymous hero
Who died like lightning
Amidst the ooze of sinew and machinery.

A Prodigal Birth in Yorkshire

I was the prodigal birth who
Arrived.
Far from the family home;
Delivered by a mother, eager
To escape the crushing
delusion of *Our Daily Blitz*
where hope
Was measured in seconds before
The bombs came raining
Down Without a Warning.
I was
Safe

For a while

In a tranquil place

Where the meadow larks

 Sang in peaceful repose,

Away
From the daily carnage
Bombarding the skeletal ruins
Of our cities and towns

The Prodigal's Progress

To the castle born, even if it was only a maternity home for evacuated mothers to deliver away from the bombs and sirens of our blitzed cities. Yes I was born in a castle, Hazlewood Castle just outside Tadcaster in Yorkshire & I have my birth certificate if you need proof However as the years passed I was convinced that I was born in the castle in a small image on the back of a pack of Players Navy Cut cigarettes. I must have told others this falsehood many times over the years because my Dad smoked them & he wouldn't have lied! But eventually I discovered that it was an illustration of Nottingham Castle and the legend of Robin Hood that had surfaced in my boyhood dreams became another castle. Regardless, I knew for sure that a blue flow had coursed through my veins over the years. Therefore my DNA must have had a royal connection somewhere over the centuries and my birth certificate still says Hazlewood Castle.

Obviously it is hard to claim that I remember those early years during wartime except for the stories of my survival when the bombs fell near the houses I lived in. Therefore when I was told that an incendiary bomb came down on my crib and killed my teddy bear, it still gave me a funny sense of loss and uncertainty about all those friends who have left me, including those stuffed animals. They must be looking down on me still because my prodigal progress has kept me in touch with these memories as I wander the world trying to find my home with its familial roots and connections. And I am still looking.

I am NOT America

But I am a friend, a foreigner,
Perhaps an alien,
Who lives across the lake
In the Cold White North
Where igloos and beavers
Welcome your summer explorers
Carrying skis on their campers
In search of snow in July.
For over 50 years I have followed
Your career with keen interest
Questioning, appreciating
Criticizing and commending
Your intensity.

It began in England when I was a boy
Who was told that your chewing gum
Was a hazard when swallowed
That would wind around my windpipe
And choke my national pride.
As for your blue jeans
They were sailcloth best used on boats, not people
For I had short pants and a uniform.
I still believed that *Tizer* was *the Appetizer*,
That tea was better than *Coca Cola*
And that *Cadburys* was the very best chocolate
Even if a *Mars* bar was my secret favourite.
HP sauce slopped over my cabbage and potatoes
While ketchup was still a novelty
And *Wimpy* burgers were yet to be born.
Even peanut butter could not compete with
Bread and jam on a smoggy afternoon.

Yes, you had been a visitor

Even a defender of my land
Who had overwhelmed us with
Your generosity and jitterbug jive.
Along with Sinatra, Goodman and Miller
By moonlight,
You handed out silk stockings to our maidens
Who had come to serenade before duty called them back
The following day.
We thanked you for the gifts
But you left a hole in our hopes when you moved
Into Europe to face the Iron Curtain,
Leaving us rationed and weary.
Yes, you left us some bases
To defend what or who, I never knew
Because *The Daily Worker* was on our news-stands too
And soapbox socialists were screaming
"Give Stalin a chance, we want peace,
Send the Yanks home"
in Hyde Park on a Sunday afternoon.

My schoolboy curiosity needed to know you better.
Were you the good guy or the bad guy?
Cowboy or Indian, Billy the Kid or Wyatt Earp,
Crazy Horse or the 7th Cavalry at Custer's last stand
In the cinema *a la* Errol fighting redskins or defending
The Saxon forests from bad King John and the sheriff,
While Burt's *Crimson Pirate* swung around the castle walls.
Your films were an endless parade of Saturday morning matinees
With Buster Crabbe and Johnny Weissmuller defending
My freedom in the desert and the jungle,
As Hopalong, Gabby, Roy or Gene appeared
On a mountain top waiting for Lash, Tom or Flash
To free me from the savages of a pot-boiling tribe
Or an Evil Empire from some distant galaxy.
You fed me nonstop

With heroes and heroines
Friends and villains

Fables and fantasies
Skyscrapers and big, big cars
That crossed over your endless horizon.

At the White City Stadium
Your athletes convinced me
That you ran faster, jumped higher
And threw a discus over the moon
Except for the Jamaican sprinters and Zatopek
Who brought you down to earth occasionally
You boxed Cockell, Turpin and Mills off our front page
With a Louis, a Robinson or a Marciano
Showing me your strength, your skill and determination
To win another golden belt.

You had meat and gravy on the table,
While I rationed through my childhood
On fried bread and dripping sandwiches.
your vision was bright and large
Sometimes too good to be true
 Because I saw those pictures of the lynchings
And hooded KKK ghost riders burning the crosses
Of oppression on you coloured folk.
I wondered
How you lived with such horrors?
Yes, your magazines showed me
 The rich and the famous,
The poor and the destitute,

The glamorous and the profane,
The gangsters and the saints.
Not to mention Johnnie Ray crying
Or Frankie Laine whistling on the wind
We called the West End.
Or seeing *Oklahoma* come alive with chicks and ducks
That scurried through the waving wheat
As tall as an elephant's eye
Before Annie fired her gun.

Yes you were big, so big in fact
That we joined you in Korea
Where our glorious Gloucesters were surrounded
And one of your generals offered a permanent solution,
An A or H bomb to blast a permanent hole
In the Commie hordes.
It didn't happen.
But you did give him a paper parade before
He faded away, shrouded in the Stars and Stripes,
Smoking a corn cob pipe as a folk hero
Or the last of a dying breed.
In fact
I even bought a book on Chiswick High Street
Called *Ordeal by Fire*
With portraits and pictures,
Battle plans and lists
Describing your Civil War.
My floor became the new battlefield
When I pulled out a tin cowboy, a mediaeval knight
And a pirate from my toy box.
Robert E. and Ulysses S. were dressed for war
At Antietam and Gettysburg on my bedroom floor
While Sherman marched past my fireplace on his way
To Georgia even if he didn't really give a damn.

Then there was Joe McCarthy ranting under the lights
While the Rosenbergs faced the flashing bulbs
Before a wagon sent them to hell, leaving me with
Visions and questions I could not understand.
Maybe the Commies had to be stopped
With the FBI rounding up the bad guys on TV
Just like in the movies when you sent Cagney to the Chair.
Thank God you gave me the Bowery Boys though
Fighting for freedom down at Louis'
With Leo G. smacking some sense into Huntz
Before saving America one more time.

Then you went golfing with Dwight
And you began enjoying the suburban weather

With Betty Crocker in your kitchen
While you drove to work
In your Chevrolet.
I was ready for more as I passed your embassy in the Square
On my way to Canada House with a short visit to Farm Street church
Where my father had sung the *Ave Maria* to your socialites, as a boy.
So when 1956 arrived I'd really know what you were doing.

Found Poem (Sheridan Sun) March, 1976 U.S. Speakers Out class Canadians

Someone from the U.S.

Is someone who has...
Something worthwhile to say

Is someone who is...
An entertainer

Is someone who has...
A much softer line

Is someone who is...
Much easier

Is someone who has...
The American style

Is someone who is...
Free for the day

Is someone who has...
Buster Crabbe(s)

Is someone who is...
One of Hollywood's Tarzans

Is someone who has...
An ignorance of Who's Who in Canada

Is someone who is...
Procuring Hot Lips

Is someone who has ...
Approached her directly
(at her home address)

Is someone who has...
Bandwagon popularity

Is someone who is...
Calling the shots

Is someone who derives...
His livelihood from it

Is someone from the U.S.

On Looking at a Piece of Tinfoil After Burning It in 1962

I see a crisp world amidst this flux
Which tells of creation, time and unity
Once seen amongst the stars
I see a God whose hands
Made land, sea and tree
But what do I see?

I see Man cut out squarely
On a sheet of doom
Telling the onlooker
He sees ME
A statistic carved out of
Bell,
Book
And candle
Asking me to smell
A flower
Before the mushroom
Takes its place
Amongst the symbols of
Eternity

On Looking at a Piece of Tinfoil After Burning It in 1973

I see a bright world amidst this flux
Shimmering magic moments
Transcending time.
A single shining star
On an ocean of black velvet.

Visions of forests burning
Before my eyes
A small crackle bursting
With the energy of a
Thousand suns
Like brilliant inspirations
For a song of fiery love
Yet to be consumed
Amidst the vastness of my
Mind.

Author's Notes written in December, 1974

This poem was written in a classroom after visiting the vacant lot area behind some portables. I found a piece of discarded, rusty old iron rod which had been left behind forever until I came along and began to give it. a new meaning with my words. The opportunity to cause a mutual understanding and relationship with this garbage-I feel is part of the poet's craft namely the ability to humanize (personify) the inanimate object with a series of stark and clearly chosen, word images. My personality evolved in and through a recognition and feeling for this object. I call this experience creative osmosis whereby my words permeate the membrane of the iron rod and give it a distinct personality. In a sense I have become one with the object I am writing about. I have used my imagination, curiosity and passion to recreate the content in my own style.

Readers can judge whether I succeeded in my stated goal or not.

MJW, September, 1998.

Living or Dead
Staked to a weed
Just waiting to die
Rusty old iron
Crippled and bent,
Performing no deed,
I pulled you from rubbish.
NOW
Shapely and turned,
Textured and curved,
Cushioned in orange,
Stark in relief
Sculptured forever,
Born in my head
Strong or fragile,
You live in my eyes
Your past is my curiosity
Covered in dreams.
Iron support for mighty spaces

OR
Wrecking rod of
Criminal intent
Kept for a moment
To be writ and read.
Mangled obscurity
Immortalized in
RED.

In Memoriam: Gone but not forgotten

New names, new places, new faces
With old stories and old memories
Always asking,
"Why am I here and
Where am I going?"

Doce me to endure....When I cry
Doce me to serve.......Without a lie
Doce me to love.........Without asking why
Doce me to survive....Before I die

Once my friends were make believe
Found only in my dreams,
While I slumped upon a lumpy mattress
Beneath an industrial, chemical sky
Where neon lights lit the avenues
On stormy summer nights,
Before another June bug
Attacked the humming, spinning fan
And died.
Sleepless moments without relief
With only a flickering Black & White television
Delivering '50s fun on another humid night.

Meus pater qui es(t) in terra debitoribus
Mon pere qui es(t) in caelis

I didn't know, nor did I care.
Forgive me for all the years
I gave you only my ridicule and blame,
Delivering my shame without love
During so many penniless days.
Watching a grown man turn cold and gray,
Shoveling a neighbour's snow
to pay our rent
Or mowing another lawn
to feed my hungry face.

Lest I Forget

LEST I FORGET

I begin to touch
The faded photos gathering dust
Around my living room floor,
Picturing the lives of those
Beyond these walls
Who answered the call,

ENLIST

Never mind what for.
Becoming another story
Remembered by a fool.
Where death was glorious
Only in the pages of my books,
While heroes died daily,
Not lucky or unlucky
BUT
Only dead.

AL WAYS & FOREVER BECOMING

Collateral memories
For the folks back home.

Newly traumatized
                          tragic heroes
Who linger daily,
                          and nightly too
With those frightful thoughts
                          that never rest.
Life long casualties
Saluting the poppy every year,
While wearing wounds that never heal
Before the columns of chiseled names
Decorating our memorial walls.

What Good is Friday

What good is Friday

When protesting, Arabs' blood flows
Like oil over corrupt, desert lands,

When worldwide poverty spreads
With unrelenting, selfish shame,

When health care regularly consumes
Our fragile lives with new, unpaid bills,

When engulfing tsunami storms appear
Along with rig spills in the sea,

When our spring loaded rivers burst again
Unchecked and flood the native towns,

When our verdant forests begin to die
Under stifling clouds of man- made fire,

When our flowers continually wilt
With the withering colours of decay,

When a child's gifted egg becomes
Only another broken, empty shell,

When a hardworking family has to crawl
Through another abandoned company town,

When our best schools close
Their doors to the penniless poor,

When our hard earned sweat papers
The walls of a bankrupt schemer's vault,

When sartorial, T.V. saviours deliver
Mass produced icons for a miracle cure,

When polaroid Poker stars click and gamble
By playing games with our addictions,

When Jersey's Atlantic shore resembles
The background, glitter of a burlesque, variety show,

When a wedding royally celebrates its
Everlasting love with rows of Asian porcelain,

When cerebral, media twits encourage
Another sensational, inflated ego to trump over us,

When poll made, politicians profess
Under duress to seek our trust,

When Sunday finally arrives
And the Sun forgot to rise,

What good is Friday
When the Sun forgot to shine?

Music Tapes: Chet Baker

Once upon a time,
In a far away place
I met a man with a horn
Blowing soft notes in the air.
His face was filled with love and care
And I asked him if he could share
His sounds so fair
He looked down and said,
"Listen son, I've got a story to tell
That you should know.
I lost my way long, long ago
And I ran from my home
With nowhere to go."

My mom said,
"Don't go son"

But I said,
"Hell, I need some fun,
You got too many rules
And I am young.
So, so long mom,
I'll give you a call
Or send you a card
When I'm done"

The city's bright lights gave me a scare
The bus rumbled slowly and turned at the station
And when the engine stalled
I was alone with my pack
And a sandwich half eaten in its wrap.

Shuffling on,
A bright light shone
At the **Y**
A room for the night.

A place to hide,
A place to mind
When the fun would begin.

Night sleep with nightmares in my dreams.

"I want my mom"

"Shut up kid, go to sleep
you're not paid to shout.
Shut up before I knock you out"

"Mom, what do I do?
Where am I?
Where do I go?

Too bad son, it's all yours now
But we'll see you coming back,
I'm sure."

Riding through waves of rocky sleep
Then waking to find my pack was gone,
A golden trumpet was resting by my bed.
On the table a dried out sandwich sat
As only a green sandwich can,
With a neon flickering through my window
Announcing the dawn.
A truck rumbling by outside
Dropping papers on the curb,
Steaming vents blowing in the morning light.

Come blow your horn

Swinging down to my place,
Rocking and sliding to the sounds
Of honking cars and screeching tires
With the skyscrapers hovering
Over the breaking day.

Come blow your horn

Walking along the endless pavement
Counting the cracks along the way.

Block after block
Of traffic lights and cars,
Buses and trucks,
Pigeons flying.
And seagulls swooping down
To scoop a mackerel's head
Down at the Fulton market
With the fishmongers yelling
As the fish continue smiling,
Sliding across from Louie's restaurant
Where the morning chowder
Is consuming the air.

Come blow your horn

Parading in the middle of town
The confetti is flying,
The president is coming.
The people standing by on cement
And concrete joy.
A little kid finding a dime,
A soldier saluting the flag
Beside a tree standing tall
On Fifth Avenue.

Come blow your horn

Down in Chinatown,
Red, yellow signs inviting me
To fathom the menu,
While little men rushing by,
Filling their carts with vegetables and swine,
A cop coming along the avenue
Swinging his stick and singing a song.

Come blow your horn

At the Flatiron Lunch
That's ringing with chat
And chomping cigars,
Smoked meat and fries

Are flying with flair and care
From loudmouthed waitresses
Counting on tips in their minds.

Come blow your horn

To the evening, flashing tiger's eyes
From neon lights of parading flesh
On voyeurs walking in a daze,
Slot machines ringing
Garbage droppings on the floor,
Bells singing a winning score,
With tin cans spinning past needles
That have broken the law.

Come blow your horn

Old man snuggling down
On a cardboard mattress
Searching for a bed
Of warm night air
Issuing from the bowels of the dead
Roaring with transit fury in his head.

Come blow your horn

Riding around the park
With Love in the air
Going to the Met
Below a beam of tranquil light
Dancing with the trees,
Shadows in the night
Serenading my hopes and dreams.

Come blow your horn.

Seurat's Sunday Afternoon

Dots and dots and dots
Making shape and substance
And sense from
Segments of separation
Moving in ripples
Of people
      Watching
Colour
      Watching
Barking dogs
      Watching
Children chase butterflies
While little girls
Smell fresh flowers
And watch sail boats sail
Along glass green menageries.

Shape without motion
Motion without form
Structured and timeless
Eternally still like toys
In a store
Waiting to be wound
And anticipating their steps
Along parasol avenues
Where shadows unveil
The activity of now
Before the key winds down
With a final flash.

The Traveling Companions by A.L. Egg

Rattling along
To the music of Browning
She sits in her crinolines
Counting the time
While her sister dreams
Of the ocean
They have left.
The village in the sky
Where the fish follow
The rainbows
And sing with their fins
In the dripping nets
Of fishermen
Who worked with toil
Before ascending the hill again
To a welcoming rest.

Poised in mirror like pose
Conveying the memories of yesterday
When blue waters caressed their youth
While sailors winked
To tease their blushes.
Gone is that time
For like the train of conformity
They return to their home
Where dresses and etiquette
Will consume their days.

Van Eyck's Marriage Ceremony

Marrriage of mannequins
Permanently costumed
In yesterday's dust
Holding the hand of wax
Extended forever
With a cherished emerald
Reflected in a mirror
Walking backwards
To eternity.

Magritte

Skies, rocks and the doves
Devour the rippling waves
That crash along the shore
Hovering above in a spiritual sleep
Of brooding finality
That steams and drifts away
Before another roar
Repeats its journey
To the shore.

Trains Near Murnau

Children chugging
And choo, chooing
Around the nursery walls
Watching trains foam and spit
Puffing clouds
Over sesame fields of hay
Where lambs live
Beside the farmyard gate.

Serious steel engines
Whirling down the telegraph wires
With a rhythmic rat a tat, tat.

Canaletto's London

Handel's music sings through
Your barges and spires
In heavenly praise
As every stroke ripples
Along the Thames water
Your sky's an endless horizon.
But around the next corner
Hogarth's rogues observe
A new Belinda
Taking a fall
When left too long
In front of a mirror
Which forgot to reflect
The reality of time.

Madonna by Munch

No virgin purity shrouds your white body
But like a swirling temptress
appearing only on wintry nights
you consummate my
fantasies.

Black and blue storms surround
your immaculate
deception
as I journey closer to your lips,
Fearing that you will grip
my obsession with vampire's lust.

Then to see your gentle repose
of cool, persuasive charm,
My feverish desire to cloister your body
In a nunnery that only hears
The chaotic chorus of midnight birds
Swirling and twirling in a manger
Is my reward at journey's end.

The Lady of Shalott

An Arthurian beauty wandering
along the lakes and rivers of legend,
a flower child floating through forests and streams
of magic encounters with knights and toads
and butterflies and daisies.
Your hair of wisp like bliss
favouring conclusions from your onlookers
extending their hands
to touch your ethereal grace
before magical garlands entangle them.

You are gone before you are caught
because the oar that's dipped in your pool
reflects the mystery that shrouds your purity.

Your candles are calling beacons
to a bed that drifts on waves of air
through forests and fields
Delivering us again to your soft couch
for a mystical kiss.
Before drifting away and
Leaving us alone and lingering.

I Live in the Memories

I live in the memories
Of yesterday when I was small
And had so much
To dream,

I live in the memories
Of when I was young
And placed my heart
On a theme,

I live in the memories
Of my family
Who grew in a home
Where love was supreme,

I live in the memories
Of my life
Filled by friends
Who shared in a scheme,

I live in the memories
Of the places I have been
Capturing the images
Of mountains and a stream,

I live in the memories
Of what has been.
Before I leave
On a celestial sunbeam.

Vignettes:
Reading Pictures & Seeing Words

Stone Staircase
Symmetrical and parallel
Yellow stone fading into nowhere
Beyond the dark mystery
At the top of where
An elfin grove of delight
That shines on me
In the forlorn woods of now.
No concern can master my footsteps
As I march along the path
And mount the steps
To my resurrection.

Carcass
Bleached dry bones
Remind us of yesterday
When you pranced through
Moss and rock and fern
With blood rushing fury
A fur lined, feline predator
Of nature's domain.
Now you caress a rocky plateau
With airy majesty
A sentinel of death
Delivered from life
To live in an onlooker's memory

Red Leaves
Blood transfusions, corporeal flesh
Drooping in a sunglow autumn.
Juice laden crimson
Bobulating on a stem
Of tender fragility

The brilliant mask of
A tree awaiting the naked abuse
Of a winter storm.

The Space Shuttle
If kangaroos do it,
Why not man?
Ride a unicorn to the Galactic Fair
Traveling along the celestial highway
Before waving goodbye to the gnomes
Down there
And fly through the sky
To parts unknown
Glistening in air
Before you become a carousel
At the fair
Blast off now boundless and free.

Grunge Rock Singer
Prophet of doom
Magician with sound
Chameleon with renown
Whose life echoes
With percussive concussions
And vibrates through
Concert hall darkness.
Caress our hopes
And shroud our gloom
With a lively tune.

Rock Group
The rays above your heads
Are like the lasers
In my mind
Your energy rebounds
With a golden hue
And shatters the void
That separates me
From the throttling mob

That gestures wildly
At your feet.

Old Man by a Fence
Can I see your hands
And count the hooks
You pulled as fresh flesh
From the ocean's harvest?
Your cold condition tells me now
That memories and fences
Are enough for one
Who toiled in earnest
Now go and God bless you
For it's time to rest.

Harbour Boats at Midnight
Twinkle, twinkle little stars
The boats are out tonight
Lovely lake, lantern light
And make mine mink tonight.
Friendly rest is best
Come on in
And be my guest

Night Sky over Water
Colour my life with madness and hope
And accelerate my heart
To catch a sparkle
Before the shroud of night
Defines my extremities.
Give me a whisper of serenity
Before I sleep.

Tiny Shack
When I was a boy
I lived in a toy house
With windows and a door.
Now that I am older
I live in a house

With windows and a door
But the problem is
I cannot sleep.
Gingerbread man why are you gone?

Snow Landscape
Cool and lingering smoke
Puffs across my memory
As I wander
In the nicotine free air
Of our winter's grace.
Dressed in a blanket
Of calm fragility,
Warming my virility
Before the storm
Blows away
My sincerity.

Misty Lodge
A journey into mystery
Clasping the pines
In a foggy coat of serenity.
Weary from walks
Through mongoose pools
Of white gases
That gather around the memories
Where nothing is mist.

Yellow Model
Swish and sway yellow butterfly
Dance and prance about my studio
Penetrate my lens
And give me the power
To invade your privacy
Before you fly along
To your next flower.
Eyes of the cat,
Sharp and fine
Intent to challenge

My tranquility
On winter days.

Venice Grand Canal
Houses stacked like Lego
Along the sidewalk bank
The water glitters
And gathers around
The choral voices
Singing a sacred tune.

Horse in Florence
An old bag of hay
The pigeon fodder
Of Italian urchins
Who beg for your crumbs
Amidst the splendour
Of ancient stones.

Iron Gate at Versailles
Sunlit iron of glistening majesty
A motif to marvel
The corrugated conquest
Of destiny's horizon
Sun god supreme
Because time is like the sand.

Lafayette's Ceiling
Caught in time
Your tentacles thrust out
To the jewel at your hub,
A purple crystal that perfumes
The air above in a gentle repose.

Model
Luscious, lascivious adventure
Into mysteries of negligee visions.
Lime green fruit
That silk touches

Before the master consummates
Your canvas in passionate abandon.

Clouds on a Gray Evening
Gloomy, cold and damp decisions
Force me to leave before
A wind rustles in my bones
And with arthritic assurance
Tells me that to endure
Is enough for now.
Cold, gray sky
Open to the light
And let my hope
Remain an horizon away.

Red Racing Car
Streamlined, sublime
Shiny and fine
Belly of the whale,
Bullet of the shark,
Fin of the fish
Poised in crimson fire
Under a parasol shade
Fire engine fire,
Roar and rev
Before we are dead.

Spider's Web
Tentacles of fire
Clasping the window panes
Shame is a ruby
That knows no master
It is a menu of maybes
Yet to be delivered.

Sunset in Venice
Solitary joy celebrating the hereafter
A bobbing smudge on the spire
Of transcendence

With a wavy crystal
That caresses the shore.

Concrete poetry- The Window
Visions of rain
Cascade my imagination
And while the petals of a flower
Command my attention
Rain splashes on my windowsill
Answering the when of where
I left my umbrella.

Canoe on Water
Joyful peace under a tranquil sky
Barking fire into rumbling azure
Screaming passion on still calm
Ripple, hooking, silver fish
In northern line.
Man alone pulling his paddle
To catch his hearth
At the end of day
While a solitary pine
Like a darkening shroud
Fingers the night.

Trees
Majestic trees thrust
Into the sky by day
Probing the universe
With their gentle touch.
Feeling the wind
Touching their leaves
Like the butterflies
That flutter in a meadow.

Horse Grazing
Now you're happy
Chewing the green clover.
But where were you when

I put down five dollars
On win, place or show,
With your head in front
Before a photo decided
You'd been nipped at the wire.
But never mind
How much better
It is to see you here
Resting at last
In a field with peaceful dreams.

Spanish Bull Ring
Perfect symmetry
Trumpets the show
Before blood and tears
Consume the dust.
Spectacle supreme
Gushing crimson
In the frenzy
Of a circle
With the monster arriving
As the crowd roars.
But later the meat is hung
Beside a butcher's table
For three dollars a kilo.

Sunset Trees
Chariots ride through fiery skies
Bombarding the crystal air
That gathers above the dinosaur trees
Delivering a memory for those
That wander and marvel
At the view.

Moonlit Fish Shacks
Generous and still
Your light covers us all
In the shadow
Of your tranquility

Like a spotlight
That beckons us to sleep
And wait for tomorrow's
Wakening call.

Laser Sunlight
With lightning spewing along
The sunset highway
Dividing the trees
And telegraph poles
That announce the next town,
Thundering cars shoot down
The alleys of interminable night.

Palms and Breakers
Why do you come down
On my turf, Man
While I'm lounging on the sand,
Man
Drinking my rum, Man.
You crash my sleep, Man
Waking me from my dreams,
Man
Where I love to live
In the warm sway
Of an ocean day, Man
Dancing with my lady
To the reggae rhythm
Of Marley's wailing, Man.

Cloudy Day on the Lake

The Canadian obsession
For Water and pines
Is there for all to see.
Give a Canuck a paddle,
And he'll pull
A cloudy sky.
And he'll spit

A hook,
And he'll fish.
Why do we look so Canadian?
Even Miss Canada
Once wore a Mounties' hat
At the Miss Universe pageant.

Other books & media projects by Michael J. Walsh

from **Mosaic Press**

Singing in the Mist: Collected Poems (2008)

Roughin' it in The Bush: Faded Memories & Other Journeys (2012)

Roughin' it in Kanata, Eh!: Fresh Memories & Other Journeys (2019)

A Celebration of Life in Art by Herman Falke: Editor Michael J. Walsh

from **MW Enterprises**

Media & Communications: History & Theory Workbooks Updated & Revised annually over 30 years for various college programs **(MJW)**

Foreign Languages Press (China) & creating a Comparative Arts course **(MJW)**

My Journal Notes on my trip to Poland & former East Germany in 1991 **(MJW)**

Conversations with Inving Layton on his poetry & his celebrity status. Six one hour chats filmed originally on videotape **(MJW)**

International Joint Commision)on on the Great Lakes teleconference on high & low water level & clean water, Research & editorial script suggestions fo the IJC live broadcast on October 141, 1989 **(MJW)**

Halton Professional Business Group. Team member assisting new college graduates to complete & approve their professional business plans (MJW)

Clapham College: The Boys in Blue & the Class of 54. A full colour memorial booklet collected & published by me in 2014. (MJW)

Original Quotations & Aphorisms: Unpublished **(MJW)**

The Fluddite Philosophy of Reasonable Possibilities in a Flexible Future

The Fluddite Manifesto & Its Values; unpublished **(MJW)**

Critical Essays & Opinions on finding the Truth using indigenous teachings unpublished. **(MJW)**

Josie Sciascio-Andrews says

I have had the pleasure of knowing Michael Walsh as an editor, publisher and friend since the now distant 2014. I was introduced to him when I had approached Mosaic Press about publishing my book of poems, A "Jar of Fireflies." Michael, the co-founder of the Press became the editor of my poetry collection, preparing it for publication in 2015.

After retiring from a long career as a professor in the Faculty of Animation, Arts and Design at Sheridan College, he has written two volumes of his memoirs: "Roughin' it in The Bush" and "Roughin' it in Kanata, Eh!"

Soon he will be releasing a new book of his poems, "Singing Forever in My Memories." with beautiful cover art done by his late wife, Anna Pagnello.

I am very fortunate to count Michael Walsh as a colleague and friend. He is a talented writer, editor, professor and publisher as well as a passionate and caring human being. He is a promoter of people and the arts. His writing as well as his life's work reflect the essential values of integrity, friendship, community and social justice.

A magnanimous generosity and humility downplay his place in the landscape of Canadian Literature. One of a new generation of artists & publishers in the 70s, he never forgot those who had been the industry's pioneers including Jack McClelland, Patrick Meany and Gladys Neale in Toronto and his conversations with John Calder in England. Michael Walsh still shies away from the spotlight he so much deserves after over 50 years in Canadian &International publishing.